Beautiful

Different In A World That Is The Same

SHEILA HOFFMAN

WESTBOW
PRESS®
A DIVISION OF THOMAS NELSON
& ZONDERVAN

WestBow Press books may be ordered through booksellers or by contacting:

WestBow Press
A Division of Thomas Nelson & Zondervan
1663 Liberty Drive
Bloomington, IN 47403
www.westbowpress.com
1 (866) 928-1240

ISBN: 978-1-5127-3665-6 (sc)
ISBN: 978-1-5127-3664-9 (e)

Library of Congress Control Number: 2016905421

Print information available on the last page.

WestBow Press rev. date: 04/12/2016

Dedication

To my four *beautiful* daughters, Kristen, Keli, Kari, and Kelsey. Continue to *be* the example and to *set* the standard! Be faithful to teach the nine foundational principles of this study to my sweet grandchildren, Kaitlyn, Logan, Blake, Trent, Hannah, Hope, Leah, Aubrey, and Hadley. I pray that they will *hold* the example and *retain* the standard!

Contents

Acknowledgments

Two or three years ago, God took hold of my heart and would not let go until I sat down and wrote *Beautiful*. I was reading through the pages when the Holy Spirit started speaking to me about the amount of information being presented. We had a long conversation about taking the book and creating an interactive manual with no time increments and restraints. What I thought would be a long and tedious process took less than six months. I penned it as quickly as God spoke it. The words are definitely His words. I assure you that this teacher has learned much more from this project than any of her students ever will.

The interactive manual would not exist without the love and servanthood shown by my sweet Kari. Thank you for the long hours you spent sitting in front of your computer and typing the original manuscript.

Once the book became an interactive manual, the search was on to find someone to type the second manuscript. I have often heard it said that going to the ladies' restroom is an event for women. Can I get a witness? This idea was proven to be true when I was in the ladies' restroom between two worship services and God brought my sweet sister Charlotte Akin and I together. I shared my vision with her, and immediately she made herself available. Charlotte, you are a true picture of a servant of Christ.

Special thanks to my newly found sisters at Briarwood Presbyterian Church in Birmingham, Alabama. Words cannot express what your prayers and encouragement have meant to me during this long journey. I look forward to Thursday nights when we shut out the world and enter into His presence to study the Word together.

Thank you, Jolee Wintermantel, for coming to my rescue one Thursday night when I desperately needed a computer guru to format the final manuscript. God has my vote for you if He ever wants to add "mastering computer skills" to His list of spiritual gifts.

I knew that God had smiled on me when He surprised me with my second little bundle of joy just fifteen months after my first. Thank you, sweet Keli, for that Saturday in Columbus, Georgia, when we thought that placing the images in *Beautiful* could not possibly take more than a couple of hours. Five hours later, after no shower and no lunch, we arose victorious.

* * *

Introduction

For as long as I can remember, I have lived in "Girl World." In the beginning God decided that I would be a girl and live in this world of drama and emotion. From pink blankets to zits, from makeup to boys, to raging hormones, it has truly been a roller-coaster ride of a lifetime. Sure, there were times when I was screaming, "Stop this ride and let me off!" But there were also those times when I was laughing and giggling, saying, "Father, don't ever let this ride end. I want to go again!" Not only did God fashion me into a female, but also His plan included placing four beautiful little females inside me. Yep, you guessed it. I birthed four little women over a period of eight years. And oh boy! Let me be the first to say, "Girl, that's when the drama really began!"

In 2010 three of my daughters got the word that they were expecting precious little bundles of joy. The first daughter found out that in January of 2011 she and my precious son-in-law would have a beautiful little girl. My second daughter was told that in February (yeah, that would be the month right after January) that she and her sweet husband would welcome their second little girl into their family. That left my third daughter, who was waiting to get her news from the doctor. I did not need to hear from the doctor. I had my confirmation from a much higher source. God gave me a promise, and that promise revolved around the number three. Three is the number of perfection in the Bible. God was going to send three girls to our family in five months as a confirmation of His perfect plan for me to minister to women, young and old.

I have to take a few moments to share with you why this third girl was such a miracle. My second daughter has polycystic ovarian syndrome (PCOS). Many women with PCOS have to take fertility drugs in order to have children. The syndrome and the fertility drug together can increase the chance of giving birth to a male child. My daughter had already given birth to two boys and was expecting to hear that the third was on his way; however, God had already let me know that He had another plan. The announcement of that third child, a *girl*, was my confirmation to write this study and begin a journey to reach women, young and old, with the truth of God's Word.

About the Study

I am the mother of four young women and the grandmother of six little girls. I owned cosmetic franchises for ten years and worked with over three hundred women on a daily basis. I have been a featured speaker on skin care and cosmetics at national and international seminars. I have had the privilege of working with many beautiful women over the years. One central truth that surfaced time after time was this: beautiful women more often than not are very insecure. Who they are and the way people see them is wrapped up in how they look. A wrinkle or a zit would appear, making the beautiful woman's world quickly come to an end. In the kingdom of God, beauty is whom you look to. In the world's kingdom, however, it is all about a person's outward appearance. In God's kingdom, it is all about His inward presence.

God started tugging at my heart with this word *beautiful*. Beauty is something that many girls and women think about often. It is on many magazine covers and on many television commercials. It is at the center of our conversations at school, work, and play—and even in our churches. I wanted to take this word *beautiful* and, letter by letter, use it to discover together truths in God's Word that can empower us and change us forever. Each verse that we will study is one that must be read, claimed, and memorized. These verses must be in our arsenal so that we will be ready to deal with challenges and difficulties that we will face in life.

Being confident that a work has been started in us and knowing that it will be completed gives us peace and purpose. Everything we say and everything we do must show the world that our hope lies in One who can and will do abundantly beyond what we can ask or think. We must trust in the Lord, knowing that He has a plan for each of us, a plan for hope and a future. And, finally, we must strip off the sins that slow us down and run with endurance this race that God has set before us.

I chose not to use time increments or restraints in this particular study. I want the Holy Spirit to guide you through this journey. I do not want you to feel pressure to complete a certain section by a particular day or week; however, the most effective environment to choose for completing this study is a group setting. If you are participating in a group study, you may be given an assignment by your leader each week so that everyone will be able to participate in the group discussion.

Each section begins with a letter and a corresponding Bible verse. You can work through the exercises as your schedule permits. Remember: you will never *have* time to get in the Word. There is always something else to do. You must *make* time to get in God's Word. We do what we want to do. When getting with God is our first priority, everything else falls into place. God made that promise to us in Matthew 6:33 when He said, "Seek first My kingdom and My righteousness, and all these things will be added to you." What things? All things! When God has first place in our lives, everything else we need, and a lot of what we want, will fall into place. If we try to do it on our own, then we will fail! Without Him we can do nothing (John 15:5). I challenge you to seek Him first, at the beginning of each day. If you do, then I promise you that you will have more strength and more energy to face what comes your way. God created us to have fellowship with Him, yet often we do not find time in our day to meet with Him. Just as we cannot grow and mature without physical food, we will not grow and mature in Christ without spiritual food.

At the end of this study I have included, in a format that can be taken with you in your purse or posted on the dashboard of your car or on the mirror in your bathroom, all the verses discussed within these pages. This will make it easier for you to memorize the Scriptures and be more familiar with their meanings. I will share a helpful hint with you that has helped me memorize Scripture in the past: repeat the verse five times each day for one week. At the end of the week, I had—just as you will have—that verse memorized.

We must hide the Word of God in our hearts. Psalm 119:11 tells us to hide His Word in our hearts so that we will not sin against Him. Do not ever make the mistake of thinking that you live in a nation where your Bible cannot be taken away. We are taking God out of everything in this country. When you take God out, precious one, there is nothing left that is good. Hide His Word! Memorize it! People cannot take away what has been hidden in your heart.

In this study we will use many translations of the Bible. This is because at times we can read the Word but not understand what it is saying. Have you been there? I have—many times. It is during those times that I am very thankful for the faithful people who have been led by the Holy Spirit to translate God's Word into a simple, easy-to-read form.

I pray that God's Word will come alive in the pages of this study. I believe that the Bible is God-breathed! It is His personal love letter to us, His children. The King of Kings has revealed Himself to us in every verse, in every passage. When selecting the verses used in this book, I first read the verses in every Bible translation and then chose the one that was easiest to understand. I am listing the different translations below along with their abbreviations so you can easily recognize from which translation each verse is taken.

AB—The Amplified Bible

HCSB—Holman Christian Standard Bible

MSG—The Message

NASB—New American Standard Bible

NIV—New International Version

NLT—New Living Translation

Take my hand, sweet sister; we will make this journey together. We will invest many hours in God's Word, and because of that investment we will never be the same. We will never again look at beauty in the way we did before. We will never again make the mistake of thinking that beauty is skin-deep. We will discover through God's Word, and through the time we spend together, that true beauty—eternal beauty—comes from the One who lives within. We will let our light shine before others so that they will see our good deeds and glorify our Father in heaven. We will refuse to hide our light under a bushel any longer.

I am asking God to raise up an army of young women who will love God with all their heart, soul, mind, and strength; women who will arm themselves with the sword of the Spirit and the shield of faith; women who will march with me into the Enemy's camp and take back everything he has stolen; women who will be pure because God is pure; women who will stand for truth because God is truth. If you are weak and cowardly, do not enlist in this army. I am asking God for warriors—mighty warriors who can join with me to change what is happening in their city, their state, their country, and their world. We must believe that the God who lives in us is greater than the god of this world. We must march forward into battle knowing that if God is for us, no one can stand against us. Satan has already been judged and condemned. We are awaiting his execution. He knows that his time is short. His wrath in these last days will be great. The Evil One steals, kills, and destroys. Do *not* be one of his victims! Be alert! Stand firm in the faith! Be strong and courageous! God came to give you life, abundant life. Here it is, precious one. You may experience blessings or a curse, good or evil, life or death. God says, "You choose!" Choose blessing. Choose life!

You are in my thoughts and my prayers.

How to Use the Study

When God birthed these nine foundational stones into my life, I knew He had given them to me to share with others. I knew these principles needed to be taught through an interactive study. I chose not to use the traditional format of weekly and daily lessons. Many of us have busy schedules and may not be able to spend one to two hours each day in the Word. I wanted the Holy Spirit to be free to guide you through each page and each section in His time.

There are several different ways, as follows, that this study can be used to learn these nine principles and then share them with others.

1. Individually
   You can choose to work through this interactive study on your own. Pray and ask the Holy Spirit to speak to you as you work through each page. You will deal with sensitive issues such as bullying, relationships, depression, and suicide. Answer the questions truthfully. Be honest. God knows your heart. Get your feelings out in the open and allow the Holy Spirit to bring healing and comfort.

2. Mother and Daughter(s)
   As the mom of four daughters, I always made sure that my girls had a devotional guide readily available to them at all times. Knowing that money might be tight and that purchasing a devotional might not have been at the top of their list as teenagers, I paid for any Christian material I felt like they might need. Many times they would see my growth as I worked through a certain devotional, and as a result they would ask for that particular study. I look back and have many sweet memories of working through a study together and laughing and crying as we grew and learned how to live like Christ.

3. Community
   Men seem to find time to get together for hunting, fishing, or watching a ball game. Women wear many hats, such as being wife, mother, daughter, cook, and housekeeper—and the list goes on. We often do not make it a priority to have girl time. We need that time to get with other women and share our challenges and experiences. Satan uses isolation to attack and defeat us. There is definitely strength in numbers when it comes to God's warfare. Pray about having two hours of girl time in your home twice a month. Don't wait until you have the time. That will never happen. You must make the time to get with your friends in order to pray and study together and become that army of women who are willing to stand in the gap for their families.

4. Church

This interactive study shares passages of Scripture that every Christian must know and understand to have the solid foundation that God needs to build His superstructure. These passages teach nine principles we must strive to apply to our lives every day if we are to be what God has called us to be.

1. "Be confident He has started a work and He will finish it" (Philippians 1:6 NIV).
2. "Everything you say must be good and helpful so that your words encourage those who hear them" (Ephesians 4:29–30 NLT).
3. "And we know that God causes all things to work together for good to those who love Him and to those who are called to His purpose" (Romans 8:28 NASB).
4. "Unto Him who is able to do far more abundantly beyond all that we ask or think, to Him be glory in the church and in Christ Jesus forever and ever" (Ephesians 3:20–21 NASB).
5. "Trust in the Lord with all your heart. Do not lean on your own understanding. Do not be wise in your own eyes" (Proverbs 3:5–7 NASB).
6. "I urge you to offer your bodes as a living sacrifice, holy and pleasing to God—this is your spiritual act of worship" (Romans 12:1–2 NIV).
7. "'For I know the plans I have for you,' declares the Lord, 'plans to prosper you and give you hope and a future'" (Jeremiah 29:11–13 NIV).
8. "Uphold me with Your righteous right hand. I will not fear. You are my God. You will help me" (Isaiah 41:10 NASB).
9. "Let us strip off every weight that slows us down, the sin that hinders our progress. Let us run with endurance the race God has set before us" (Hebrews 12:1–2 NLT).

This interactive study is designed to be taught in a Sunday school class setting, during a Tuesday night Bible-study session, or as a Sunday evening breakout class. Assignments can be given each week depending on the material being covered and the needs of the particular group you are leading. This study is perfect for organizations that reach out to the community and share Christ with different segments of society.

B: **Be Confident**

Being confident of this, that He who began a good work in you will carry it on to completion until Jesus comes back.

—Philippians 1:6 (NIV)

You Can Have Confidence because of the Following Things:

- God created you.
- God will carry you.
- God will complete you.

Because of these three truths, we can be confident. We can live confidently, knowing that He is God!

God Created You

The Creator of the universe created you. Psalm 139:13–16 (NLT) reads as follows:

> You made all the delicate, inner parts of my body and knit me together in my mother's womb. Thank you for making me so wonderfully complex! Your workmanship is marvelous—and how well I know it. You watched me as I was being formed in utter seclusion, as I was woven together in the dark of the womb. You saw me before I was born. Every day of my life was recorded in Your book. Every moment was laid out before a single day had passed.

1. Circle every instance of *me*, *my*, and *I* in the passage above.
2. Record the total here: _____

God has planned every day for us. We can do His will if we just trust Him and let Him lead us!

Refer to Psalm 139:13–16, above, and fill in the blanks below.

You made the_____ parts of my body.

You _____ me together.

Your workmanship is _____.

Psalm 139 is telling us that God doesn't make any junk!

However, Satan paints a very different picture for us. He tells us that we are unloved and unwanted. He causes us to put the spotlight on the things about ourselves that we do not like.

No one within the sound of my voice likes everything about herself. In the space below, list the things you would change about yourself if you had the opportunity.

Two Basic Truths

1. Change what you can change.
2. Accept what you cannot change.

First Corinthians 9:27 (NIV) reads, "I beat my body and make it my slave so that after I have preached to others, I myself will not be disqualified for the prize."

Of the following two choices, check the one that applies to you. (Please be honest! Remember that only God is looking.)

_____ I am a slave to my body. I give my body what it wants when it wants it.

_____ I make my body my slave. I tell my body what it is going to have.

First Corinthians 9:27 gave me victory over my weight. I once weighed 225 pounds and wore a size 22W dress. Weight is a form of warfare. Satan wants you to be overweight, tired, and unhealthy. God gave you a strong, healthy temple. Nourish it. Take care of it. Exercise it. God's plan for you is to have an abundant life.

Which one are you choosing?

Circle the words that best describe where you are in your life right now.

Fatigue	Exercise
Eat right	Eat what I want
Good	Evil
Life	Death

Life Principle: It does not matter what you think of yourself or what others think of you, good or bad. What matters is what *God* thinks of you.

God created you, and He makes no mistakes!

God Will Carry You

In order for God to carry a person, He must have all of that person. God wants all of us. Let's look at Psalm 119:45–48 together.

Draw a line from the part of the body to the corresponding verse.

feet	Psalm 119:47
mouth	Psalm 119:45
heart	Psalm 119:48a
hands	Psalm 119:46
mind	Psalm 119:48b

Look up each verse listed below, and then fill in the blanks with the correct verb.

Psalm 119:45   I will _____ freely because I seek Your precepts.

Psalm 119:46   I will _____ of Your Word and not be ashamed.

Psalm 119:47   I will _____ in Your commands.

Psalm 119:48a   I will _____ my hands to Your commands which I love.

Psalm 119:48b   I will _____ on Your statutes.

Psalm 119 teaches us to *love* His Word, to *know* His Word, and to *hide* His Word.

The one question I am asked most as I travel and speak is, "How do I know what God's will is for my life?" I refer people who ask this of me to Psalm 119:125 (HCSB): "I am your servant; give me understanding so that I may know Your decrees."

When we become *completely submitted* to God and who He is, we gain *understanding* and *know* His Word and His *will*.

God Will Complete You

The foundation stone is salvation, knowing that you belong to Christ and that Christ belongs to you. This foundation stone has to be there so that God can build your house, your temple, for Him.

Look up the following verses, and then in your own words describe what God is saying.

John 14:6

John 10:9–10

Romans 10:9-10,13

With our _____, we believe and become righteous.

With our _____, we confess and become saved.

Be sure that you know that you know that you know that you are saved, that you have been called out of darkness and into His marvelous light. The beginning of God's work in you is salvation. He cannot complete a work He has not started.

God created you, God will carry you, and God will complete you only if you belong to Him.

If you cannot confidently say, "I am His and He is mine," please go to www. succeedandlead.org and ask us to contact you. We want to talk with you personally and send you information to help you learn how to walk in His ways. God loves you, and we love you. We are all in this battle together. To be confident and live confidently, we must spend time in His Word. His Word must consume us.

* * *

Congratulations, my sweet friend! You have completed the section centered on the first letter of a word that describes who you are and what you will become when you love God and follow after Christ with all your heart, soul, mind, and strength.

Next we will add the letter *e* and talk about your words. Do they edify and build up, or do they tear down and destroy?

Let's see what God has to say about the tongue.

B E _ _ _ _ _ _ _

E: **Everything You Say**

Everything you say must be good and helpful so that your words will be an encouragement to those who hear them. Do not use foul or abusive language. And do not bring sorrow to God's Holy Spirit by the way you live. Remember, He is the One who has identified you as His own, guaranteeing that you will be saved on the day of redemption.

—Ephesians 4:29–30 (NLT)

The verse above begins with, "Everything you say." Let's see what the Bible has to say about the tongue. Look up the following passages and then record below everything you learn about the tongue.

James 3:6 and 3:8

James 3:9–10

Psalm 34:13

Proverbs 21:23

James 1:26

1 Peter 3:10

In light of these verses, let me share four valuable points that I learned from my former pastor, Dr. Steve Gaines, in a sermon called "Simple Guidelines about Speech."

Be gentle in your speech. Proverbs 31:26 (NIV) reads, "She speaks with wisdom, and faithful instruction is on her tongue."

1. Establish two rules.

   - Speak only if the words are wise.
   - Speak only if the words are kind.

2. Think before you answer. "The heart of the righteous *ponders* how to answer. But the mouth of the wicked *pours* out evil things" (Proverbs 15:28 NASB, emphasis added). You should ponder how to answer instead of allowing things to pour out of your mouth.
3. Learn to wait so that you don't act prematurely and speak harshly.
4. Err on the side of less when it comes to words. Less is always best. Proverbs 10:19 (NLT) reads, "Don't talk too much, for it fosters sin. Be sensible and turn off the flow!"

Bullying is rampant in our schools right now. We hear frequently about teens who felt unwanted and unaccepted and who, as a result, committed suicide. The church is to be a *sanctuary* from the mean, ugly world outside. As Christians, which means people who have Christ living inside of us, we *should not* take part in bullying behavior.

Stop and think about a situation where you witnessed someone being mistreated or talked about unkindly. Write it down (you do not have to include names).

Did you initiate the negative confrontation? (Be honest, my sweet friend. God sees and knows everything.) If you were the initiator, then confess your sin to God and ask His forgiveness. Pray about going to the offended person and asking for forgiveness. Once you approach that person, let him or her know that not only does the Savior, who died for us, love him or her but also that someone of the same age, in the same school, and on the same level recognizes how special he or she really is.

Remember to be mindful of everything you say!

Write down something positive and encouraging that you can share with that person to make him or her feel good about himself or herself.

There is nothing lovable about us. There is nothing special about us. In fact, Ephesians 2 tells us that we are just like everybody else. "Once you were dead in your trespasses and sins ... *doomed forever.* You used to live just like the rest of the world ... Full of

Sin. You used to follow the passions and desires of your evil nature" (Ephesians 2:1–3 NLT, emphasis added). We were all born with an evil nature. Before we were saved by Christ, we were under God's anger—*just like everybody else!*

However, look at the next verse: "But God is rich in mercy and He loves us very much." When God comes in, you are no longer like everybody else!

Look up Ephesians 2:5–6, 2:8–10, and 2:12. Match the correct verses with the truths found below. I have done the first one for you.

Ephesians 2:5   He made us alive.

_____   He raised us up.

_____   He seated us with Him.

_____   We have been saved by grace.

_____   We are God's masterpiece.

_____   We were formerly separated from Christ.

Thank God for the two little words *but now*!

"*But now* you belong to Christ. You were far away from God; now you have been brought near to Him because of the blood of Christ" (Ephesians 2:13 NLT).

We belong to Christ. He has taken up residence in us. We are His holy habitation. He could have chosen anything to inhabit, *but He chose us!*

Fill in each of the blanks below with one of the following words:

See   Love   Touch   Walk   Listen

We are His hands, to _____ people lost and hurting.

We are His feet, to _____ in His ways.

We are His eyes, to _____ the pain and hurt around us.

We are His ears, to _____ to the needs of those among us.

We are His heart, to _____ Him, His Word, His church, and those who are unlovable and unforgivable.

A recent Christian study showed that a considerable number of dechurched people say they are willing to return to church. Sixty percent of teens and young adults said they would return to church simply if they were asked!

Read James 5:19–20 (MSG).

"My dear friend, if you know people who have wandered off from God's truth, don't write them off. Go after them. Get them back and you will have rescued precious lives from destruction and prevented an epidemic of wandering away from God."

He is a million miles away from cliques and groups that shun and exclude people just because they might be different, or dress differently or act differently, from what *we* call normal or acceptable.

Watch everything you say!

Do not bring sorrow to God's Holy Spirit by the way you live.

* * *

Way to go, young warrior! You have finished the section focusing on the second letter of a word that describes who you are and what you become when you love God and follow after Christ.

Next, we will look at the letter *a* and discover how all things work together for good when we love God and are called according to His purpose.

Let's see what God's Word has to say about passion and purpose.

B E A _ _ _ _ _ _

A: **All Things Work**

And we know that God causes *all things* to work together for good to those who love God, to those who are called according to His purpose

—Romans 8:28 (NASB, emphasis added)

All Things

Youth has a way of making us think that we are indestructible, that death is for the old and aging. When we are young, we feel like we can move mountains and slay giants with one hand tied behind our back. One stroll down the halls of a children's hospital will expose that this belief is a lie of Satan, the Father of Lies.

Write out Psalm 139:16 in the space below.

One truth we will all discover if we live long enough is that sometimes bad things happen. God uses the good things and the bad things to grow us up in Him and to complete us.

Good Things

Look up the following verses and record what God is saying about the good gifts and blessings.

James 1:17

Ezekiel 34:26

Philippians 4:19

Who meets all your needs? What resources does He use to meet those needs? Write your answers below.

Look up Philippians 3:10.

In the space below, write out the two ways in which Paul, the author of Philippians, states that he wants to know Christ.

Philippians 3:10 talks about power and sufferings. People tend to love the blessings, the power, the glory, and the victory. However, knowing Christ in the fellowship of His sufferings is not something we would choose. No one wants to suffer. Christ Himself did not want to suffer.

Let's take a walk into the garden of Gethsemane and listen to the words of our dear Savior as He talks with His Father. What did Jesus pray in Gethsemane? Let's look at Luke 22:42 (AB) to find the answer: "Father, if You are willing, remove this cup from Me, yet not My will, but *always* Yours be done."

Jesus prayed three things in this prayer.

1. "If You are _____." Jesus was fully aware of the suffering He was to face.
2. "Remove this _____." Jesus was struggling with going to the cross.
3. "Not _____ _____ but Yours, Father, always _____ _____." He chose to do His Father's will.

Look at Luke 22:44. Being in agony of mind, Jesus did what? He prayed all the more *earnestly* and *intently* until His sweat became like great clots of blood dropping down upon the ground.

When we are struggling, when we are facing problems and challenges, what must we do in order to follow our Lord's example? Write your answer below.

Let's now talk about trials and struggles. What about the bad things that happen?

Bad Things—Trials and Suffering

- Expect trials.
- Expect trials to produce joy.
- Expect trials to produce endurance.
- Expect trials to produce maturity.

Expect Trials

"I have told you these things so that in Me you have peace. In this world you will have trouble (trials and sorrows). But take heart! I have overcome the world" (John 16:33 NIV).

Expect Trials to Produce Joy

"Consider it a great joy, my brothers and sisters, whenever you experience various trials" (James 1:12 HCSB).

The phrase "whenever you experience various trials" assumes that trials or bad things are a normal part of the Christian life. In fact, trials are necessary if we are to be faithful disciples.

What trial or difficulty are you facing in your life right now? Write your answer in the space below.

What truths did you learn from John 16:33 and James 1:12 that will help you experience victory and become a faithful disciple? Write your answer below.

Are we happy when bad things happen? Are we happy when we are hurt, disappointed, or facing difficult circumstances? Of course not; however, there is a difference between joy and happiness.

Life Principle: Happiness depends on our circumstances. Joy depends on the God of our circumstances. We are joyful knowing that He loves us and is in control.

Expect Trials to Produce Endurance

Look up Romans 5:3–4 and record below the three-step process that suffering produces.

Look up James 1:12 and write down the prize we receive when we endure various trials.

The word *blessed* in James 1:12 reflects the understanding that a person who walks in the path set by our Lord sees his or her circumstances in terms of the hope that is coming, the hope that awaits us as believers.

In light of eternity, what we are going through now, no matter how hard or difficult, is only a few moments.

Expect Trials to Produce Maturity

Look up the following verses and list what the Father does for His children after they have endured suffering for a little while.

1 Peter 5:10

1 Peter 1:6–7

Hebrews 12:10–11

Discipline and suffering train us to be like Christ so that we may partake in His holiness!

All things work together for good when we love God and are called to His purpose.

God must be the source of everything we do, so how do we make God the source of everything we do?

Love God

We are all going to be passionate about something, so I suggest that you get passionate about God. List below what some people's passions, other than Christ, might be today.

Our passion defines who we are and what we will become.

Look up Mark 12:28–30 and write below which command Jesus said to the scribe was the most important command of all.

Be Called to His Purpose

What is God's purpose for us?

The salvation of Paul is recorded in Acts 26:16–18. In this passage, the Lord tells Paul exactly what he is to do now that he is saved. Those instructions to Paul are the very same instructions for us today as believers.

Read Acts 26:16–18 and write down the purpose that our Lord gives to Paul and to all of us who have been saved.

There are three parts to salvation:

1. Justification represents the past
   "He became sin who knew no sin. He canceled our debt and nailed it to the cross" (Colossians 2:14 NASB).

2. Sanctification represents the present
   "You are a chosen race, a royal priesthood, a holy nation, a people for His possession, for He has called you out of darkness into His light" (1 Peter 2:9 NASB).

3. Glorification represents the future
   Please read Revelation 21:1–7. You will be blessed and encouraged by it, as it was written for you.

For a better understanding of this process of justification, sanctification, and glorification, please complete the exercise below. Write the name of the particular step of the three-part process of salvation that best describes each statement below.

_____ I will be saved from sin's presence.

_____ I have been saved from sin's penalty.

_____ I am being saved from sin's power.

* * *

Congratulations, precious one! Now you have a better understanding of why bad things happen to God's people. Believe me, this is a truth you will have the opportunity to share many times with your friends and loved ones. Knowing that our suffering produces joy, endurance, and maturity will strengthen us so that we may persevere and trust that God is causing all these things to work together for our good.

Let's look at the letter *u* and find out more about the power and provision we have as God's children.

B E A U _ _ _ _ _

U: Unto Him Who Is Able

Unto Him Who is able to do far more abundantly beyond all that we ask or think, according to the power that works within us, to Him be glory in the church and in Christ Jesus to all generations forever and ever. Amen.

—Ephesians 3:20–21 (NASB)

God is able to do the following things:

- Strengthen us, as we have His power
- Provide for us, as we have His provision
- Protect us, as we have His protection

The Power of God

Look up the following verses and write down what each one has to say about the power of God.

Romans 1:16

1 Corinthians 1:18

1 Corinthians 1:24

Complete the exercise below to discover more about God's power. Fill in the blanks using the list of words and phrases provided.

giant   virgin   created   chosen vessel   delivered   trust

1. God's power _____ the universe.

2. God's power _____ the children of Israel out of bondage.

3. God's power brought down a _____ because of a little boy's faith and _____ in his God.

4. God's power took a simple _____from a small village and used her as the _____ _____ to carry the Savior.

Let's take those truths and relate them to our lives.

1. God's power created you.
2. God's power can deliver you out of any bondage that you might be struggling with.
3. God's power can bring down any giant in your life when you trust God and exercise faith.
4. God's power can take you, a simple girl from a small town or a big city, and use you as the chosen vessel to carry the love of your Savior to a lost, dying, and confused world.

O precious one, my eyes are filled with tears as I write these words to you today. This awesome and great God took time to fashion and create me. That same God empowers me and makes me more than a conqueror. Bondage is not God's plan for me. He came to give me life abundant. And where the Spirit of the Lord is, there is freedom.

Let's look at the verses below and dance before the Lord as David did in 2 Samuel 6:14: "David was dancing before the Lord with all his might." Read each verse below and record what God is saying to you about your freedom.

Galatians 5:1

John 8:32

John 8:36

Romans 8:15

2 Corinthians 3:17

We have God's power because of God's provision. Read Acts 1:8 and fill in the blanks below.

But you will receive _____ when the _____ _____ has come upon you, and you shall be my _____.

What has God given to us to empower us?

You were told to tell others. You were saved to lead others to Jesus, your Savior. This is your purpose! This is why you live and breathe, why you are given the gift of life every day—to be like Jesus, not like others.

Look up the following verses concerning the Holy Spirit, the promise given to us as believers. Record the different names given to the Holy Spirit along with the various methods the Holy Spirit uses to empower us.

John 16:7

John 14:16–17

John 14:26

John 16:8

John 16:13

Embrace this incredibly amazing gift given to you by your sweet Jesus. Take hold of this promise given to you by your loving heavenly Father. The Spirit replaces Jesus's physical presence by permanently dwelling within the blood-bought followers of Christ.

"You, however, are not in the flesh, but in the Spirit, since the Spirit of God lives in you. But if anyone does not have the Spirit of Christ, he does not belong to Him" (Romans 8:9 HCSB).

"The Spirit Himself testifies together with our spirit that we are God's children, and if children, also heirs—heirs of God and coheirs with Christ—seeing that we suffer with Him so that we may also be glorified with Him" (Romans 8:16–17 HCSB).

Write down three persons of the Trinity.

1. The _____

2. The _____

3. The _____ _____

Complete the sentences below by identifying the person of the Trinity and the purpose each one serves.

The Trinity

The _____ sent His Son to be sin for us, to cancel the debt we owe that we cannot pay. The _____ died for us and was raised up to give us victory over death. Jesus now sits at the right hand of the Father and prays for us.

The Son sent the _____ _____ to us to guide us and to teach us all truths.

Embrace the Holy Spirit, the third person of the Trinity. Do not be afraid of Him. He is part of the divine plan God has for all of us who belong to Him. The Holy Spirit is the means by which we are adopted into God's family.

"All of those led by God's Spirit are God's sons" (Romans 8:14 HCSB). Hallelujah! *We have God's protection because we belong to Him.*

"I am not ashamed. I know whom I have believed. I am convinced that He is able to guard what I have entrusted to Him until He returns" (2 Timothy 1:12 NASB).

What have we entrusted to Him?

Look at what Paul says: "I know whom I have believed." It is our faith, our belief, that we have entrusted to Him. It is this faith and this belief that we must guard day by day until He returns.

What has He entrusted to us?

"Guard, through the Holy Spirit who dwells in us, the treasure which has been entrusted to you" (2 Timothy 1:14 NASB).

What is this treasure that has been entrusted to us? Look up the verses below and complete the sentences to discover the treasure.

Psalm 119:11 (NIV, NLT): I have _____ Your _____ in my heart, that I might not sin against You.

Psalm 40:8 (NIV, NLT): Your _____ is written on my _____.

The treasure entrusted to us is the gospel, God's Word. Either sin will keep you from His Book or His Book will keep you from sin.

To live a holy and righteous life, we must hide His Word in our hearts. To know God's will and plan for our life, we must allow His instruction to live within us.

We have God's power, we have God's provision, and we have God's protection, because He is able! *He is able to do exceeding abundantly beyond what we can ask or think!*

There is nothing you can ask that God cannot do. There is nothing you can think that God cannot make happen when it is His will.

Look up the verses listed below and write them in the space provided.

Jeremiah 32:17

Jeremiah 32:27

What statement appears in both of these verses?

What challenges or difficulties are you facing right now? What has you bound up and defeated?

Precious one, write out Ephesians 3:20–21 in the space provided. Jump up and down on it! Claim it! Tie a knot in it and hang on! Rest in His promise that nothing is too difficult for Him.

Write it out and memorize it!

He can and will do exceeding abundantly *beyond* what we ask or think! Hallelujah!

Write out a prayer of thanksgiving to God for His power that strengthens you. Thank Him for sending His Son to pay the debt you could not pay. Thank Him for providing the Holy Spirit to guide us and to teach us His truth.

God will bless your faithfulness in studying His Word. We are in this fight together, sweet sister. Let's move forward and learn how to put our trust in the One who will never leave us or forsake us.

B E A U T _ _ _ _

T: **Trust in the Lord**

Trust in the Lord with all your heart. And do not lean on your own understanding. In all your ways acknowledge Him, and He will make your paths straight. Do not be wise in your own eyes. Fear the Lord and turn away from evil.

—Proverbs 3:5–7 (NASB)

To trust anything or anyone other than the Lord results in disaster.

- We cannot trust in riches. Read Proverbs 11:28, and then fill in the blank below.
  Anyone trusting in his _____ will fall.

- We cannot trust in self. Read Proverbs 28:26, and then fill in the blank below.
  The one who trusts in _____ is a fool, but one who walks in wisdom will be safe.

- We cannot trust in our beauty or how we look. Read Proverbs 31:30, and then fill in the blank below.
  Charm is deceptive and _____ is fleeting, but a woman who fears the Lord will be praised.

- We cannot trust our friends. Read Micah 7:5, and then fill in the blank below.
  Do not rely on a _____. Do not trust a close companion.

- Refer to Jeremiah 9:4 to fill in the blank below.
  Everyone has to be on guard against his _____.

- Read Jeremiah 9:5 in order to fill in the blanks below.

  _____ deceives _____. No one tells the truth.

Now I want to talk about friends. If I meet your friends, I will know exactly what kind of person you are. I do not even have to meet you. Friends have an amazing influence on who you are.

The Institute in Basic Life Principles teaches that there are four levels of friendship, as follows.

1. Acquaintance

   A. Defined as an occasional contact

   B. Involves asking general questions

      - Where do you go to school?
      - Where do you live?

   C. As a Christian, we must see every new acquaintance as a divine appointment.

2. Casual Friendship

   A. Look for common interests and activities

   B. Talk about goals and opinions

   C. Identify positive character traits

   D. Observe for oneness of soul (the mind, the will, and the emotions).

3. Close Friendship

   A. Involves oneness of spirit

   B. Involves sharing the same life goals

   C. Involves praying daily for each other

   D. Involves memorizing Scripture together

4. Intimate Friendship

   A. Identified as the deepest level of friendship

   B. Involves helping each other mature in god-like character

   C. Defined by honesty, humility, and discretion

   D. Involves praying for one another.

   E. Involves encouraging one another to pursue spiritual maturity.

Let's hit the pause button and put this information to practical use. Hopefully, you are now looking at the people you know through the eyes of Christ. After completing this section on friends, you may have been convicted about some of the friendships you are currently involved in.

Prayerfully complete the exercise below. Look at the different levels of friendship. Write below each one the names of your friends who would meet the qualifications discussed earlier.

Acquaintances

Casual Friendship

Close Friendship

Intimate Friendship

You may have discovered that some of your close friendships really need to be more casual. You may need to spend less time with friends with whom you do not have a oneness of spirit.

Look at people you meet through the eyes of Christ. Pray and seek God's direction in your relationships. Ask God to give you friends with whom you can share Scripture. Pray with friends who will encourage you to be more like Christ.

Jesus was surrounded by the multitudes. He chose twelve with whom He would have a oneness of spirit, twelve with whom He could share Scripture and pray. He had only three (Peter, James, and James's brother John) with Him at Gethsemane. You will not have many intimate friends.

The material below is from the Institute in Basic Life Principles:

> You will have many acquaintances and casual friendships with both believers and nonbelievers. However, true fellowship requires that both persons share the same life goals. Friends influence our lives daily. They encourage us to

pursue a closer walk with God or discourage us from following Christ. Every believer should make three basic decisions about friendships:

1. Let God choose your friends based on their desire for God's best. True friends exhort and encourage one another.
2. Purpose to verbally identify with Christ. Learn to stand alone against evil. Do not compromise. With a loving and meek spirit, explain, "I belong to Christ and I cannot do that."
3. Realize that those who reject Christ should reject you. You should not have intimate friendships with nonbelievers because you do not share the same life goals. The one who walks with the wise will become wise, but a companion of fools will suffer harm (Proverbs 13:20).[1]

Stop now and pray about your relationships. Go to the *Prayer* section in the back of your manual and write out a prayer of commitment to God that from this time forward you will let Him choose your friends. Commit your life and your relationships completely to Him. God does not accept partial allegiance from His children. He wants all of us. Jesus paid our debt in full with His blood on the cross. We belong only to Him!

Remember the following:

- "To trust anything or anyone other than the Lord results in disaster" (Proverbs 3:5 HCSB).
- "Do not be wise in your own eyes" (Proverbs 3:7 NIV).
- "Do not be proud. Associate with the humble. Do not be wise in your own estimation" (Romans 12:16 HCSB).

Let's look at the life of Jesus as described in Philippians 2. I love this passage of God's Word because it presents a beautiful picture of the servanthood of my dear Savior. I often refer to this passage as the servant chapter in the Bible. I often pray this over my children and grandchildren.

Write out Philippians 2:5.

In this verse *mind* is interchangeable with attitude. You must have the same mindset, the same attitude, the same approach to life that is in Christ Jesus. You are what you think. How you think determines how you live.

---

[1]   "What Are the Four Levels of Friendship?", Institute in Basic Life Principles, accessed January 17, 2016, http://iblp.org/questions/what-are-four-levels-friendship.

Right thoughts lead to right actions. Wrong thoughts lead to wrong actions. Once you are thinking right, you can start living right.

Write out Romans 8:6.

The attitude mentioned in Philippians 2:5 brings true peace with God. To stay at peace with God, we must do the following things:

1. Confess our sins and stay clean (1 John 1:9).
2. Pray about everything (Philippians 4:6–7).
3. Live in the Word of God (Psalm 119:165).
   Those who love the Word of God have great peace. Nothing causes them to stumble.
4. Focus your thoughts on Jesus.
   "You will keep the mind that is dependent on You in perfect peace for it is trusting in You" (Isaiah 26:3 HCSB).
5. Cast your cares on Jesus.
   "Cast your burden on the Lord and He will sustain you. He will never allow the righteous to be shaken" (Psalm 55:22 NASB).

We *must* do the following things:

- Trust in the Lord.
- Rely on His wisdom.
- Think about Him constantly.
- Let Him be our guide.
- Refrain from considering ourselves to be wise.
- Let His mind be in us.
- Stay at peace with Him.

I wish I could come to where you are right now and give you a great big bear hug. This has been an intense lesson, with a lot of information and exercises that may have been personally challenging. You may need to go back through the material again and take a few moments to let it all soak in. I imagine that you've read some information you hadn't ever encountered before.

I want to encourage you to look at relationships differently in the future. Ask God to give you friends who will build your life and challenge you to be like Christ.

Determine in your heart today that you will be the one who does the *influencing* in your close and intimate friendships, not the one *being* influenced.

Trust only in the Lord! Trust Him for right relationships. Trust Him for right thoughts. Once you are thinking right, you can live right!

Press on, dear sister! In Romans 12, what is God urging us to do? Let's move on to the letter *i* and see what God wants us to do with these beautiful bodies He has given to us.

B E A U T I _ _ _

/: I Urge You

> I urge you, brothers and sisters, in view of God's mercy, to offer your bodies as living sacrifices, holy and pleasing to God—this is your spiritual act of worship. Do not conform any longer to the pattern of this world, but be transformed by the renewing of your mind. Then you will be able to test and approve what God's will is—His good, pleasing and perfect will.
>
> —Romans 12:1–2 (NIV)

I urge you to present your body as a living sacrifice. This means that you must dedicate your *whole* life to living for God's honor. Christians are to be different from non-Christians. The world is in the church today to such an extent that God's Word and God's truth have become what *we* say it is and how *we* interpret it. The world says that nothing is absolute, that everything is relative. We water down the truth until things are no longer black and white, no longer right and wrong.

However, I love my God! He is sovereign! He is absolute! He is black and white—no gray. He leaves no room for error or misinterpretation.

Let's talk about our bodies for a minute. God made boys, girls, men, and women to be different. It was His plan. That is why homosexuality goes against everything that God stands for. I say this with a heart full of love for homosexuals and lesbians. God created *every* person in *His own image*, according to Genesis 1:27.

Sexual impurity is a sin. Idol worship is a sin. Adultery is a sin. Greed is a sin. Drunkenness is a sin. Homosexuality is a sin.

God loves the sinner, but He hates the sin. We must love the sinner and hate the sin too.

If you struggle with homosexual tendencies today, please talk with a person who is teaching this study—or contact us at www.succeedandlead.org. We love homosexuals and lesbians. There is deliverance through God's Word for every sin we face. We want to share God's love and God's Word with you. Homosexuality is not part of your genetic makeup, as God has never created and never will create a lesbian or a homosexual man.

We can look at the creation story in Genesis and see that God made males and females in different ways. Let's look at the first book in the Bible, where it all began, to discover how the creation process for man was different from the creation process for woman.

Look up Genesis 2:7 and write it out in the space below.

We see from this verse that God *formed* a human being out of dust. He created a man.

Let's look at Genesis 2:22 (NASB, emphasis added): "The Lord God *fashioned* into a woman the rib which He had taken from the man and brought her to the man."

God *created* man, but He *fashioned* woman.

God made females curvy and soft, and with breasts and hips, for a reason. God Himself, not Hollywood, not MTV, and not *Seventeen*, did that!

But as females we abuse His plan. We don't consult God about what we should do with these breasts, with these hips, and with our shiny hair or soft skin. *We* do what *we* want to do. The problem with that philosophy is that our choice affects not only us but also the boys and men around us.

Our life is not our own. If you want to live for yourself, if you want to do what you want to do, then do not get saved! Do not ask Jesus to come live inside you. You see, when God comes in, you are no longer like everybody else! Remember that Jesus paid a debt He did not owe because you owed a debt you could not pay. Once you receive His gift of salvation, you belong to Him.

Write Ephesians 2:1–3 in the space provided.

Look at the list below and circle the *italicized* words from the passage that you wrote out above.

You were *dead*. You were *doomed*. You were of *full of sin*. You were *obeying Satan*. You were under *God's anger, just like everybody else!*

Thank God for the first two little words of verse 4: "But God." We were just like everybody else. *But* when God comes in, you are no longer like everybody else!

Write out Ephesians 2:5–6 in the space below.

Look at the list below and circle the capitalized words you find there that are also in the passage you have just recorded.

- MADE us alive
- RAISED us up
- SEATED us with Him

Because we belong to Christ, we *cannot* conform to this world. We *cannot* be like the world. We must be transformed!

Jesus Transforms Our Attitude

Write out Philippians 4:4–5 in the space below.

When you are saved, the *moment* you are saved, you become a citizen of heaven. You have a heavenly allegiance. You can face life with a positive attitude of pressing on and refusing to quit. The victory has already been won for you at the cross. You are living *from* victory, not moving *toward* victory. *Think like it! Live like it!*

Jesus Transforms Our Emotions

Write Philippians 4:6–7 in the space below.

As females, we are emotional beings. God made us that way. Knowing that we are emotionally driven, we must guard our thought life and realize that the mind is the battlefield for the Devil!

Write James 1:13–16 in the space below.

In James 1:15 we see that lustful thoughts will give birth to sin. And when sin is finished, it brings forth death.

Lust → Sin → Death

Lust is not, and *never* will be, love. We *must* understand the difference.

> Love says "wait"; lust says "go."
>
> Lust says "yes"; love says "no."
>
> Love says "trust"; lust says "try."
>
> Love says "life"; lust says "die."
>
> Love is God; lust is sin.
>
> Lust tears down; love always wins.
>
> —Sheila Hoffman

God created love. God also created sex. That is very evident in the Song of Solomon in the Bible. He has a plan, His plan. Don't miss it. It is the only plan that leads to a future and a hope.

At the end of this section, you will find a poem titled "Sweet Sixteen" that I wrote for one of my daughters on her sixteenth birthday. It is a prayer I pray for all my daughters and granddaughters, and for you, sweet sister.

Jesus Transforms Our Thoughts

Second Corinthians 10:5 instructs us to take every thought captive so that we may obey Christ.

Write Philippians 4:8 (NLT) in the space provided.

Circle the seven things God commands us to think about. It is not a coincidence that seven is the number of completion and perfection in the Bible. The mind is changed by prayer, by reading and reflecting on God's Word, by worship, and by meditating on who God is.

Write Ephesians 4:14–15 (NLT) in the space below.

Write Ephesians 4:22–24 (NLT) in this space.

Instead is a word found in both of these passages. Find it and circle it.

Look at Ephesians 4:30 and write down how we can bring sorrow to God's Holy Spirit.

Jesus Transforms Our Values

Write out Philippians 4:11–12. Circle the word *learned* in both verses.

"I *have learned*." We do not suddenly get contentment; *we learn it!* We lose so much when we refuse to *learn* from our experiences with God.

Paul had education. Paul had wealth. Paul had position. Paul had it all by the world's standard of measuring success and contentment.

I want Paul to tell you himself what his final conclusion was. Write Philippians 3:7–9 in the space below. Circle the words *worthless* or *less* and *garbage* or *rubbish*, depending on your translation.

What is important to you—education, wealth, position, beauty, being accepted, being the best?

Wanting these things and working for these things is not wrong as long as we keep the scale balanced and realize that everything we gain is worthless compared to the priceless gain of knowing Jesus as Lord.

Keep your values in check. When you look at everybody else, what you are doing and becoming may not look so bad.

When you look at Jesus and God's Word, when you use His life as your standard and His Word as your measuring rod, you will quickly realize that you are nothing and *He is everything!*

* * *

How exciting! We are rounding third base and are headed for home. God is a rewarder of those who diligently study His Word. It takes great discipline and courage to choose to study God's Word over doing other activities that many of your friends may be engaging in. Do not get tired of doing what is good, sweet sister. Do not get discouraged and give up, for you will reap a harvest of blessing at the appropriate time (Galatians 6:9).

Next, after you read my poem "Sweet Sixteen," we will study a Bible verse beginning with the letter *f* to find out what God's plan is for us as His children.

How is your growth and development? Are you properly nourished? We will answer these questions and more as we continue to study together.

B E A U T I F _ _

Sweet Sixteen

A little babe
Just yesterday.
Time marched on.
A teen today.

Many questions,
Many fears,
Many doubts,
Many tears.

Pressures mount
Day by day.
Friends are saying to
Try the world's way.

Do not listen.
Do not stray.
Trusting Jesus
Is the way.

Staying pure
In God's sight,
Living daily
In His light.

Dressed in white,
You'll walk one day
Down an aisle.
A man will say,

"What a beauty.
She's my queen.
In her life
Christ can be seen."

Look in his eyes
With no shame.
Pure and spotless,
Take his name.

That first night,
Just you and he,
O how special
It will be.

All those friends
Will fade away.
Before their God
They'll stand one day.

Those teenage years
Will quickly pass.
What's done for Christ
Is all that lasts.

Live for Jesus.
Let Him lead.
He is all
You'll ever need.

Give your love
to just one man.
Know God's Word;
Follow His plan.

Lead your friends;
Don't let them stray.
Show them Jesus
Every day.

F: **For I Know**

"For I know the plans I have for you," declares the Lord, "plans to prosper you and not to harm you, plans to give you hope and a future. Then you will call upon Me and come and pray to Me, and I will listen to you. You will seek Me and find Me when you seek Me with all your heart."

—Jeremiah 29:11–13 (NIV)

Three Things We See in the Above Verse

    A. God has a plan for you.

    B. God listens to you when you call.

    C. God reveals Himself to you.

I have an amazing truth to share with you today: you are *always* in God's thoughts!

Write out the following verses and circle the words *thought* and *thinking* along with any pronouns (e.g., *they, them, me, my, I*).

Psalm 40:17

Psalm 139:17–18

Isaiah 55:8–9

Read Isaiah 55:6–7 and write in the space below all the instructions given to us as God's children.

    1.

    2.

3.

4.

God spends all His time thinking about you! How much of your time every day do you spend thinking about Him? Look at your daily activities, the things you are involved in. Is God a priority? Does He have a place of respect and prominence in your life? If not, confess that sin to God. Ask His forgiveness and tell Him that you will meet with Him on a daily basis. Determine in your heart that your mind will *not* be led astray from your sincere and pure devotion to Christ (2 Corinthians 11:3). Write your prayer of commitment below.

Pleasing Him should be your life's ambition. See 2 Corinthians 5:9. This verse will cause you to stop and reconsider your behavior, the way you dress, your attitudes, your desires, and even the use of your time and money.

A Plan to Prosper

Read Psalm 1:1–3 and write in the space below what we are to delight in if we are going to be happy and prosperous.

A Plan for Hope

We see in Romans 5:2–5 that we must rejoice when we run into problems and trials because they are good for us. Read this passage and record below the steps we go through during those trials in order to grow up and become mature in Christ.

If we are going to know Christ, we must know Him not only in the power of His resurrection but also in the fellowship of His sufferings. Write out Philippians 3:10 in the space below.

So, dear sister, God not only has a special plan just for you, but also He listens to you when you call.

God Listens to You

What an exciting promise! What an amazing Word to us that as God's children we have access to the very ear of God Himself. We can cry "Abba, Father," and He will hear our voice. He knows us by name.

Write out Exodus 33:17.

We must come into God's presence every day. Moses knew that there was power in God's presence. He would not go anywhere unless God was going to be there. Look up the verses below. Write the letter of the verse in the space next to the truth being taught.

A. Exodus 33:14

B. Exodus 33:15

C. Exodus 33:16

D. Exodus 33:17

_____ There is rest where His presence is.

_____ He knows us by name.

_____ We must be different if we are to belong to Him.

_____ If God is not there, I do not want to be there.

There is a divine adequacy in the Almighty God. There is no boundary to His presence. He never loses power. He is always strong. God is never tired, and He never tires of us. Hallelujah! Get passionate about being in God's presence! Get passionate about prayer!

F 4

Learn How to Pray

    A. Be specific. Learn how to pray Scripture back to God, claiming His promises for every challenge you are facing.

- God, You said, "Call to me and I will answer you and show you things that you do not know" (Jeremiah 33:3 NASB).
- Lord, You promised that all things will work together for my good if I will love You and be called to Your purpose (Romans 8:28).

Look up the following verses and write them out as a prayer to your Father, claiming His promise for difficulties you may be facing.

- 1 Peter 5:7

- Psalm 37:4

- 1 John 1:9

- 2 Timothy 1:7

    B. Be bold. Realize your position. You have been adopted into God's family. You are royalty, the King's kid. Act like it, live like it, and pray like it!

The following verses tell us that we can boldly approach His throne. Read each one and write down what happens as the result of exercising faith.

- Hebrews 4:16

- Ephesians 3:12

- Matthew 17:20

C. Be persistent. Let's look at 1 Thessalonians 5:17 in three different translations. Memorize it! Claim it! It is dynamite in a small package. Fill in the blank with the correct word to finish the verse.

Pray without _____. (NASB)   Continually

Pray _____. (NIV)   Keep

_____ on praying. (NLT)   Ceasing

God not only listens to you but also reveals Himself to you!

David knew the importance of prayer and true repentance. Let's look at Psalm 51:10–12. Write below the six things for which David cried out to God so that he could experience true repentance and come into right standing with His Father.

1.

2.

3.

4.

5.

6.

When God creates a new heart, when God renews a spirit, and when God restores joy, the result is as follows:

1. The person will engage in Bible study.
2. The person will spend time in praise and worship of God.
3. The person will take part in ministering to others.

Let's talk about Bible study. We cannot find God unless we seek Him, and we cannot seek Him unless we spend time in His Word and get to know Him. *Love* is spelled this way: t-i-m-e.

God wants not only to save us but also to bring us to the position of adult sons and daughters in His family. He has given us the instruction manual, but we will never grow unless we diligently appropriate and apply what He has given us.

Let's look at the different stages of growth and development in the physical world. Look at the list below and put the entries into the proper order, using the numbers 1–8.

_____ Kindergarten

_____ Toddler

_____ Adult

_____ Elementary-schooler

_____ Baby

_____ High-schooler

_____ Preschooler

_____ Middle-schooler

How does a child grow from baby to preschooler? What does it take? It takes *nourishment*. This is physical development. If children do not receive proper nutrition, they will not grow and reach the next level. They will not be healthy. They will not grow and mature properly.

The spiritual body is no different. When you are born into the body of Christ, you are a baby. You are a newborn believer in Jesus.

We start out with John 3:16, the milk of the Word. But we must progress from milk to the meat of the Word as we grow in Christ. This is spiritual development. In Hebrews 5–6, God is very straightforward about the growth He expects from His children.

Let's look at these two passages of Hebrews together. Read each one and write down what God has to say about infancy and maturity in Christ.

Hebrews 5:12–14

Hebrews 6:1–3

We must go from drinking milk to eating meat. We must practice and train if we are going to enter the battle. The key to maturity in Christ is to study the Bible for ourselves. When we get into the Scriptures ourselves, we get into the meat, the solid food that produces spiritual development.

Worshiping on Sunday morning is not enough. We cannot develop by eating just one meal a week. Attending Bible study on Wednesday night is not enough either.

We must move from spiritual infancy to spiritual adulthood. God has made us responsible for our growth. At the judgment seat of Christ, we will be examined as believers in regard to our growth. We must not be lazy or indifferent concerning our growth.

"For the eyes of Yahweh roam throughout the earth to show Himself strong for those whose hearts are *completely* His" (2 Chronicles 16:9 HCSB, emphasis added).

Have you made Him the king of your heart? Do you belong completely to Him?

I am very proud of you, dear sister. If you are reading these words, you are truly growing from infancy to adulthood in Christ. You are on the threshold of completing this study. God is watching. He is sitting on His throne and saying, "Well done, little one. You are My beloved daughter; in you I am well pleased."

I am excited about the next section of our study because we will be looking at fear and worry, two things we all deal with on a daily basis in our Christian walk.

Come and join me at the *u*. I will be waiting.

B E A U T I F U _

U: Uphold Me

Uphold me with Your righteous right hand. I will not fear for You are with me. I will not anxiously look about for You are my God. You will strengthen me. You will help me.

—Isaiah 41:10 (NASB)

We should focus on two statements in the verse above:

- I will not fear.
- I will not worry.

I Will Not Fear

Satan is the Enemy. His one mission is to seek and destroy. The only way to resist him is to stand firm in your faith. Of all the names and titles used for the Devil, none is used more than "Satan." The name Satan is found fifty-four times in the Old and New Testaments, while *Devil* is used thirty-four times, only in the New Testament.

You must know your Enemy in order to defeat him. Satan studies and investigates you. He knows the buttons to push to frustrate and discourage you. You must understand what God's Word has to say about this Enemy and the power you have over him. "Greater is He that is in you than he that is in the world" (1 John 4:4 NASB).

Know Your Enemy

God has warned us to be alert and serious when it comes to our adversary the Devil. In His Word, God has revealed exactly who Satan is and how Satan works. Let's look at the verses below. Write in the space provided the name and description given for the Devil in each verse.

1 Peter 5:8–9

Acts 13:10

John 8:44

John 12:31

1 John 5:19

Write out 1 John 3:7–10. Underline the description of God's children. Circle the description of the Devil's children.

The purpose for the revelation of Jesus Christ is also given in this passage. You will discover that purpose by answering the following question: what did the Son of God come to destroy?

When we forsake sin and refuse to do wrong, we disarm the Devil and further God's kingdom. "Not able to sin" in verse 9 means we are free from the bondage of breaking God's law. We are free to live as God's children. We are not sinless and perfect, but we desire to live a life *fully* surrendered to God.

Look up Hebrews 2:14–15 and record below what the death of Jesus accomplished.

We are flesh and blood. That is why Jesus had to be born of a virgin in a manger. He had to be both human and God. The Son of God became a man and suffered death so that He could destroy the one holding the power of death—the Devil. It is because of Christ's death on our behalf that we are free from the fear of death.

First Peter 5:6–9 gives us the recipe for victory over the Enemy. List the four steps below.

1.

2.

3.

4.

God is sovereign! Satan cannot do a thing without God's permission. Satan's primary target is not those who are already deceived or lulled into apathy. It is the righteous who concern him. If you are not running into Satan head-on, then you are running the same way as he is. Satan is aware of those who truly live for God. He sees them as a threat to his kingdom.

The lion may roar and you may start to tremble, but remember 2 Timothy 1:7. Write it in the space below. Memorize it! You will need it as you battle with Satan day after day.

We do not have to fear when we know and understand the *plans* of our Enemy. We do not have to fear when we know and understand the *power* of our God!

Know your Enemy!

Be Armed and Ready

Satan is strong, but he is not strong enough to resist God! God has given you His Spirit, the same one who, through Jesus, cast out demons. He has given you His sword, the Word of God. And He has given you a direct line to His throne room, through prayer.

In Ephesians 3:14–19, Paul prays five specific things for us as believers. Read this passage and write out the Scripture reference beside Paul's petition.

_____ 1. That we would be strengthened with power

_____ 2. That Christ would dwell in our hearts

_____ 3. That we would be able to comprehend who God is

_____ 4. That we would know the love of Christ

_____ 5. That we would be filled with the fullness of God

You need not fear the Enemy. Just fear God. To fear God means you have a reverential trust *in* and an awesome respect *for* Him! If you truly fear God, you will not allow yourself to fear the Enemy.

So, sweet sister, stand up with me right now—wherever you are—raise your hands to heaven, and make this promise to God your Father: I give all my fear to You, God. I will trust only in You! I will not fear!

I Will Not Worry

"What is worry? Anything that steals your joy … something you cannot change, something you are not responsible for, something you are unable to control, something or someone who frightens you, something that keeps you awake when you should be asleep."[2]

Stop for a moment and write below all the worries you have right now. Please do not hurry through this exercise. Think about those things that steal your joy, those things you cannot control, and those things that keep you awake at night.

Now take all those worries on your worry list and put them on your prayer list. Give each worry one by one to God.

In his book *Laugh Again*, Charles R. Swindoll references Philippians 4:4–7 to give us a practical application of remedies for this disease called worry. Match the correct Scripture reference with the remedy by drawing a line from one to the other.

        Rejoice   Philippians 4:6

        Relax   Philippians 4:7

        Rest   Philippians 4:4

Rejoice

To rejoice is a scriptural command. To ignore it is to disobey God. Surround yourself with positive people. Find Christian friends who see life through the eyes of Christ. *Choose joy!*

---

[2] Charles R. Swindoll, *Maybe It's Time to … Laugh Again* (Nashville: Thomas Nelson, 1992), 200.

Relax

Let's look at Philippians 4:6. Prayer is described as a worshipful attitude; petition, as a need; and requests, as specific concerns. Thanksgiving is described as something that shapes our prayers, layering them with gratitude.

It is impossible to worship and worry at the same time. Let your worry drive you to worship. Either your worship will keep you from worry or your worry will keep you from worship!

Rest

Philippians 4:7 gives us a promise that the peace of God will guard our hearts and minds as we live in Christ Jesus. Look up Colossians 3:15–16, and then answer the following questions.

What are we to *let* rule in our hearts?

What are we to *let* richly dwell within us?

Let is an interesting word that is used in both verses. *Let* means that the matter at hand presents us with a choice. You may not be able to control *what* happens to you, but if you are in Christ you can control *how* you react and respond.

Colossians 3 talks about the peace of God and immediately thereafter instructs us to let the Word of Christ dwell in us.

Look up Hebrews 4:11–12 and answer the following questions.

What are we to enter into as God's children?

How is the Word of God described in verse 12?

Hebrews 4 talks about entering His rest. Immediately after that, it talks about the Word of God as being living and active.

All throughout the Word we can see how God's peace comes to us—by being saturated with His Word.

Worry is an enemy of joy! Worry forces us to focus on the wrong things. Rather than looking at the *known* blessings that God provides *today*, we worry about the *unknown* and uncertain events of tomorrow.

Make this pledge with me right now, precious sister: "I will worry about nothing. I will pray about everything."

* * *

It is sad to think that our journey together is coming to an end. We are moving on to the last letter, which will complete the amazing word *beautiful*.

Let's finish strong together as we learn how to run this race that God has set before us.

B E A <u>U</u> T I F U L

L: Let Us Run the Race

Let us strip off every weight that slows us down, especially the sin that so easily hinders our progress. Let us run with endurance the race that God has set before us. We do this by keeping our eyes on Jesus, on whom our faith depends from start to finish.

— Hebrews 12:1–2 (NLT)

The Flesh versus the Spirit

You cannot run the race until you identify the sins in your life that slow you down and hinder your progress in your Christian walk.

In Galatians 5, God actually lists the works of the flesh for us. Let's look at verses 19–21. Verse 19 (NLT) reads, "When you follow the desires of your sinful nature, your lives will produce these evil results":

Sexual immorality	Jealousy
Impure thoughts	Outbursts of anger
Eagerness for lustful pleasure	Selfish ambition
Idolatry	Divisions
Demonic activity	Envy
Hostility	Drunkenness
Quarreling	Wild parties

Feeling that everyone is wrong except those in your own little group

This next exercise will require you to be completely honest with God and yourself. Take off the mask that you have been hiding behind. It is just you and God. No one else is looking. The first step to true freedom is to realize that you are bound, held captive by Satan and sin. Read through the above list again and circle every sin that you are struggling with in your life right now. Remember, sweet sister, to be completely honest!

In the previous lesson we learned that when we forsake sin and refuse to do wrong, we disarm the Devil and further God's kingdom.

We will never be sinless or perfect, but we must desire to live a life *fully surrendered* to God.

Let's look at Galatians 5:21 (NLT): "I will tell you again, as I have before, that anyone living that sort of life [it is a lifestyle] will not inherit the Kingdom of God."

We are going to sin because we have a sinful nature. But in addition to that sinful nature, we have a spiritual nature. The sins you struggle with, the ones that you circled in the previous exercise, must not become a *lifestyle*. You can have victory over your sinful nature.

Write out Galatians 5:24 in the space below. Memorize it! Claim it!

In Galatians 5:19–21, we see the evil results of following the desires of our sinful nature.

In Galatians 5:22–23, God spells out for us the results of being controlled by the Holy Spirit. Read this verse and list the fruit of the Spirit below.

When the Holy Spirit *controls* our lives, He will produce this kind of fruit in us. Galatians 5:25 (NLT, emphasis added) reads, "If we are living now by the Holy Spirit, let us follow the Holy Spirit's leading in *every part* of our lives."

Have you given everything to Jesus? Does He truly live in every part of your life? Stop for a moment and look at your life right now. Are you being controlled by the flesh or by the Spirit? The former offers death, and the latter offers life and peace. *You choose, dear sister!*

Get on your knees and ask God to forgive you for keeping a part of your life secret, known to no one else but you. Go to the *Prayer* section in the back of your manual and write out your prayer of commitment. Then rise up, precious one, and live like you belong to the King of Kings and Lord of Lords!

To run this race, we must understand what it is to live in the flesh and what it is to live in the Spirit.

Look up the following verses in the book of Romans and record what you learn about living in the flesh and living in the Spirit.

Romans 8:5

Romans 8:9

Romans 8:12–14

The Holy Spirit's Ministry in Our Lives

In the eighth chapter of Romans, Paul describes two kinds of people—the old man and the new man. He explains to us the two different kinds of existence, or two different "mind-sets," they both have. The outcome of the two ways of thinking is completely different—death versus life and peace.

Christians are in a new realm, for the Spirit dwells within them. The Spirit's presence is the mark of Christ's ownership. The Spirit provides life and righteousness.

The Christian is empowered by the Holy Spirit to stop doing the sinful deeds of the body. The Holy Spirit is not an agent of bondage but is instead the means of our adoption into God's family.

Look up Romans 8:15–16 and write the verses below.

What does God tell us not to be a slave to in verse 15?

We also see in verse 15 that we have been adopted into God's family. Because of that adoption, we can behave like God's own children. What can we cry out to God as His children? Write your answer below.

In verse 16, who testifies to our spirit that we are God's children? Write your answer below.

How do we live controlled by the Holy Spirit? Paul has the answer for us in 2 Timothy 1–2. Look up the Scripture references below and write the correct reference in front of the instruction given to us as believers in each verse.

Here's a helpful hint: you will use 2 Timothy 1:8 three times. Remember, all the references below are found in 2 Timothy.

I completed the first two to get you started.

1:6	2:15
1:8	2:16
1:13	2:22
2:1	2:24
2:3	

__1:6__ 1. Keep ablaze the gift of God in you.

__1:8__ 2. Do not be ashamed of Christ.

_____3. Suffer for the gospel.

_____4. Rely on the power of God.

_____5. Be strong.

_____6. Be diligent.

_____7. Be kind and patient.

_____8. Avoid empty chatter.

_____9. Listen to sound teaching.

_____10. Suffer hardship.

_____11. Pursue the following:

    A. Righteousness

    B. Faith

    C. Love

    D. Peace

In Life, You Will Have Battles

Satan is your Enemy. He is your worst nightmare! He studies you. He investigates you. He knows you better than you know yourself. He wants to defeat you. He wants to wear you down. He knows that when you are tired and weary, you are a puppet on the end of his string and therefore he may do with you as he pleases.

You must hide the Word of God in your heart and remember that you are living *from* victory, not moving *toward* victory. Christ bought and paid for your victory with His blood. Everything you will ever need can be found at the cross of Jesus Christ.

Do not listen to Satan, the Father of Lies!

Write out 2 Corinthians 4:8–9 (NLT) below. Listen to the promise of victory given to you by your loving heavenly Father for every problem and challenge you will ever face.

Look closely at this victory verse and fill in the blanks below.

- I am pressed, but I am not _____.

- I am perplexed, but I do not _____.

- I am hunted down, but God never _____.

- I get knocked down, but I _____.

As a young warrior, you must memorize 2 Corinthians 4:8–9. Keep fighting the fight. Every battle you win by trusting God and exercising the power and authority given to you by Jesus Christ makes you stronger. Satan, seeing that strength and power, will often move on to a weaker target.

Life is full of battles. Learn to do battle.

I am sure you are facing personal challenges and fighting your own real battles right now. You think that you are all alone and no one understands what you are feeling. You are discouraged. These thoughts are coming right from the pit—Satan's pit.

I want to stop here and talk with you about a dangerous progression that can occur when you are facing difficulty. This progression is engineered by the Devil himself. Remember, he roams throughout the earth, seeking people whom he can devour and destroy. *Do not fall into his evil trap!*

It is true that life is not always fun and easy. There is winning, but there is also losing. There is acceptance, but there is also rejection. There is loyalty, but there is also betrayal. There is truth, but there are also lies.

If you live long enough, you will feel discouragement. Something beyond your control will hit you out of nowhere and will make you feel disheartened or crushed. *Do not stay in that discouragement!*

Remember the victory verse we learned in the last session, 2 Corinthians 4:8–9? I encouraged you to name it, claim it, and memorize it. You will not be crushed or broken. You will not give up or quit. God will never abandon you. You will get up and keep going.

Let's look at some other New Testament verses that testify to the fact that we are overcomers. Below, record what you learn about being an overcomer from each verse.

1 John 4:4

Romans 8:31

Romans 8:37

Revelation 12:11

If you do not leave the discouragement behind, you will become depressed. Depression is the second step in Satan's progressive plan to destroy you. The teenage years are a difficult period of time, with about 11 percent of teenagers developing depression by age eighteen.

Get out of that depression. Claim Philippians 4:13 (NASB, emphasis added): "I can do *all* things through Him who strengthens me." Memorize those victory verses you just identified and leave that depression behind. If you stay there, that depression will lead you to death.

Suicide

Suicide is the second leading cause of death for people ages ten to twenty-four. Each day in our nation there is an average of over fifty-four hundred suicide attempts made by young people in grades seven through twelve. Four out of five teens who attempt suicide have given clear warning signs.

Most people who commit suicide have depression. Depression affects a person's thoughts in such a way that the person doesn't see that a problem can be *overcome*.

"The person doesn't see that a problem can be *overcome*." Isn't that amazing! The victory verses you just studied testify to the fact that you are an *overcomer* through Jesus Christ. Jesus told us that in the world we would have trouble and problems, *but* (there's that sweet little three-letter word) He said that we should take courage, because He has *overcome* the world (John 16:33).

Remember: Satan is roaming throughout the earth seeking to destroy. Indeed, his purpose is to steal, kill, and destroy (John 10:10).

Following is the three-step progression Satan uses to destroy people:

Discouragement → Depression → Death

It was not in my plan to deal with depression and suicide. I did not have it written into the original *Beautiful* study. There is nothing beautiful about depression and death, about a life ending before it really begins. *But* this is not my study, and I am not in charge of the plan. I am simply the vessel. God is sending this message through this vessel to someone very special today—someone who has been or is depressed, someone who has thought about taking her life and ending it all.

God is saying to you today, my sweet sister, "I know the plans I have for you. They are plans for good and not disaster, to give you a future and a hope" (Jeremiah 29:11 NLT). "'The glory of this present house will be greater than the glory of the former house … your latter will be greater than your past and I will bring peace to this place" (Haggai 2:9 NIV).

Run to your King, precious one! Crawl into the arms of your sweet Jesus. You will find strength, love, joy, peace—everything you need. Pour your heart out to Him. Cast your cares on Him. He cares for you like no one else cares for you. He will never lie to you. He will never leave you. He will never tire of you or use you. He loves you more than He loved His own earthly life!

Go to the *Prayer* section in the back of your manual and write out a prayer to Jesus right now thanking Him for becoming sin for you. Thank Him for dying for you and then rising up out of His tomb so that you might live in that same victory. Commit your life *completely* to Him.

Get up off your knees, dear sister. Realize that we are engaged in spiritual warfare. Know your Enemy. The Spirit and the flesh are at war against each other.

When you are unsure of what to do or which way to go, you will hear His voice behind you saying, "Here is the road. Follow it." Learn to listen for His voice. Obey His direction.

You can change this world!

You will make a difference!

Do not live your life allowing no one to know that you have been here!

The world is getting darker every day. Be His light and shine in the darkness.

I believe that my generation of Christians will be persecuted. My children's generation of Christians may be jailed. My grandchildren's generation of Christians may have to die for proclaiming their faith.

We have known the power of His resurrection. We must also know the fellowship of His sufferings if we are to know Him personally and intimately.

Do not settle. Instead, soar!

* * *

Congratulations, sweet sister! You have made it through all nine letters of the word *beautiful*. It took determination and discipline. You have shown great faithfulness and commitment during this journey we've shared. God looks for those two character traits in His children. He has found both in you, and He is very pleased by it.

There is a bonus feature included with this study. Let's look at it before we pack up and go out to be His marvelous light in this dark world.

I can't wait for you to discover the amazing truths found in Deuteronomy 30. I love that chapter. It is one of my favorite passages of God's Word. I love it. And because I love you, I have to share it with you!

Bonus Feature

When the Holy Spirit was speaking to me about what to include in this study, I knew that Deuteronomy 30 had to make the list. It is one of my favorite passages of the Word of God. I had originally planned to put this section at the end of the section centered on the letter *l*. This content, however, is so vital and important that I prayed through and felt led to create a bonus feature in which to deal separately with the truths of Deuteronomy 30.

I love this passage because God sets the record straight. We muddy the waters and try to make things complicated. God, in this one chapter, makes things simple.

God gives us our choices: blessing or curse, life or death, good or evil. Then God looks at us and says, "You choose!" Let's look at these verses together and see God's instruction *to* us and His provision *for* us.

Blessing or Curse

We see the blessing and the curse in the very first verse of Deuteronomy 30. Let's look back at Deuteronomy 11:27–28 to find out exactly how God defines the blessing and the curse.

What is the blessing according to Deuteronomy 11:27?

What is the curse according to Deuteronomy 11:28?

It is simple:

_____ if you listen.

_____ if you do not listen.

Don't you just love God—so simple, so honest? He gives us no wiggle room. With Him it is black and white, no gray area. He doesn't ask us what we think or what we want. He says that we can listen or not listen, but He lets us know that each of those choices has very real consequences.

Now that we know what the blessing is and the curse is, let's go back to Deuteronomy 30 to find out how we get God's blessing on our life.

What does God say that *we* must do as His children in Deuteronomy 30:2?

_____ and _____

What does God say that *He* will do in response to our obedience (Deuteronomy 30:3)?

God has two more promises for His obedient children in Deuteronomy 30:5. What are they?

There is a land and a life that God has promised to you. You started on the right journey, but then you took a wrong turn, maybe several wrong turns. You still have the map, the instruction book. Use this map to find your way back. You can still possess your future.

He will prosper you and multiply you *more* than He did for those who have gone before you.

Before we dig deeper into Deuteronomy 30, I will share with you something that God has moved my spirit to share. I know that we all need to hear it, but there is someone special who needs this Word today.

Have you ever had someone say something mean and hurtful to you? Have you been left out of a group and made to feel like you were not special or were less important than you really are? Maybe you looked at some of the girls walking into your classroom and thought, *They are so cool. Why can't I be like them?*

I am about to share a truth with you that will change your thinking forever if you will just open up your heart and mind to the Holy Spirit. He will teach you God's view on popularity and acceptance.

Look at Isaiah 43:1. Who has formed you? Who has redeemed you? Who calls you by name?

Look a few verses ahead to Isaiah 43:21. Write this verse in the space below.

What statement does God make about His children in this verse, proving that we belong only to Him?

God made us! God formed us! We were created by Him and for Him! God redeemed us! He calls us by name. We belong only to Him. He alone is the One we must live to please. His telling us "well done" is the only "well done" we must desire to hear. It is His acceptance, His approval, that we must desire most.

Listen to what God is saying to us in 1 Peter 2:9. We are the following things:

- A chosen people
- A holy nation
- A royal priesthood
- God's own possession

Why are we these things? So that we might proclaim His name and show others the goodness of God, who called us out of darkness into His wonderful light.

Peter is teaching us that we are God's valuable possession. But as believers, we, like Jesus, will be rejected by human beings.

We cannot know Jesus only in the power of His resurrection. We must also know Him by being in fellowship with His sufferings (Philippians 3:10).

Remember the life principle you have already learned in this study. It does not matter what others think of you, good or bad. It does not matter what you think of yourself. The only thing that matters is what God thinks of you. His "well done" is what we are waiting to hear!

God loves us with an everlasting love. He will take care of those hurtful words and those feelings of rejection. To be a friend of God means to be an enemy of the world.

Let's look back at Deuteronomy 30 and find out what God says about our enemies.

Write out Deuteronomy 30:7 in the space below.

"God will take care of your enemies." What an amazing promise from our loving heavenly Father! Do not worry or fear. March on, dear sister. Fight the fight! God goes before you and behind you. Let *Him* fight your battles!

What is God reminding us of in Deuteronomy 30:8? "You will again _____ the Lord and _____ His commands." When we do those two things mentioned in verse 8, when we are obedient and obey His commands, what promise does God give to us in Deuteronomy 30:9?

God promises that we *will* be successful. He also promises that we will produce offspring. As females, we have been given the amazing opportunity to carry life inside our bodies.

Here is another life principle I want you to carry with you from this day on: decisions you make now will affect the children you will have in the future!

I know that having children and becoming a mother seems way off in the future. But, believe me, time passes quickly. James 4:14 (NIV) reads, "What is your life? You are a mist that appears for a little while and then vanishes."

The person you are becoming right now, the choices you are making, will determine the kind of woman, wife, and mother you will be one day. Our actions have consequences, and many times those consequences follow us into the future.

Commit your past, present, and future to the God of Deuteronomy 30. When we obey and observe His commands, He promises to restore us and to prosper us in everything we do.

How amazing and loving is this God that we serve. Look at the verses below to discover the secret to succeeding in the Christian life.

> Deuteronomy 30:2: Obey the Lord, heart and soul.

> Deuteronomy 30:6: Love the Lord, heart and soul.

> Deuteronomy 30:10: Turn to the Lord your God, heart and soul.

He wants all of us, heart and soul!

He wants all of us to obey Him and to let Him be all that He is through all that we are. Let's look at Deuteronomy 30:11 together.

"What I am asking you to do is not too difficult for you; it is not out of reach." In this verse, our loving heavenly Father reminds us that He is always with us and He is enough!

- Deuteronomy 30:12 – It is not in heaven.
- Deuteronomy 30:13 – It is not beyond the sea.
- Deuteronomy 30:14 – The Word is very near to you, in your mouth and in your heart, that you may obey it. The Word is always in your reach. The Word is always with you!

The key to obedience, the key to restoration, the key to possession, the key to prospering, the key to succeeding, is the Word of God.

The Word must be in our mouth and in our heart. We must know the Word and live it out before others.

Here it is, sweet girl. God sums it all up for us in Deuteronomy 30:19—*life made simple!* "I have set before you life and death, the blessing and the curse."

Look at the next directive—*choose!* What is God saying to us? "You choose!" He gives us a choice.

Choose to live. Choose to be blessed. It is simple with God. He lays it right out there. We are the ones who tend to complicate it.

What three things does God command us to do in Deuteronomy 30:16?

       _____ your God.

       _____ in His ways.

       Keep His _____.

Loving + Walking + Keeping = Living and Multiplying

Deuteronomy 30:20 – Love the Lord.

       Obey His voice.

       Hold fast to Him.

When we do our part, He promises us life and length of days.

Blessing or curse; life or death; good or evil: which will it be for you?

Remember, God says that you get to choose! Choose to live. Choose to be blessed! Choose to commit your life to Jesus, the One who knew no sin but became sin for you so that you could be made right with God through Him.

Also, choose to deny yourself. Take up your cross daily and follow Christ. He is all that you need! He is enough!

I want to leave you with Isaiah 43:1–3a (NASB).

Thus says the Lord, your Creator, O Jacob, and He who formed you, O Israel. "Do not fear, for I have redeemed you; I have called you by name, you are Mine! When you pass through the waters, I will be with you; and through the rivers, they will not overflow you. When you walk through the fire, you will not be scorched, nor will the flame burn you. For I am the Lord your God, The Holy One of Israel, your Savior."

What an incredible series of promises the Lord gives to us!

- "Do not fear, for I have redeemed you."
- "I have called you by name."
- "I will be with you."
- "You will not be scorched [by the flames]."
- "I am the Lord your God."

Isaiah 43:4–5a (NASB): "You are precious in My sight. You are honored and I love you. Do not fear—I am with you!"

Love Letter to My Sweet Sisters in Christ

Well, precious one, we have reached the finish line. How I wish I could be there with you right now. O how we would celebrate! I would throw my arms around you and give you a great big bear hug (my grandbabies tell me they love my big bear hugs). I am *very proud* of you for having the desire and discipline to see this lengthy study to completion. Completing this study was no small accomplishment for a young woman who lives in a society of microwaves and instant messaging. My eyes are filled with tears, but my heart is bursting with excitement knowing that the truths you have learned will now be lived out among a world filled with people who are lost and hurting. The beauty of my sweet Jesus will shine forth from you into the darkness to bring hope, joy, peace, and love.

Listen, sweet sister—stay in God's Word! Be diligent to present yourself approved to God as a good worker, one who does not need to be ashamed, one who correctly handles the word of truth (2 Timothy 2:15). You must study and prepare for what God has planned for you. The Christian life is truly a walk—you don't pick it up and put it down. You must *walk* in His ways. To walk in His ways, you must *know* His ways. His Word must consume you! The more time you spend in His Word, the more you will hate sin! Meditating on the Word will make you wise. It will give you understanding—understanding beyond your years. When you become *completely surrendered* to what God wants and who God is, you will have understanding and will know His Word and His will (Psalm 119:125). You are inadequate apart from the Word of God! Let the Word of Christ dwell in you. Let the Word of Christ saturate you and remain in you as a rich treasure.

Remember that the Enemy will keep coming back. Hide 2 Corinthians 4:7–10 in your heart. Don't forget that you are living *from* victory, not moving *toward* victory. All you need—all you ever will need—was bought for you at Calvary with the precious blood of Jesus. Let Him be all that He is through all that you are in every circumstance and situation. You are more than a conqueror through Him who loved you (Romans 8:37). You can speak with authority, in the name of Jesus, and as a result the mountain in your way must move. Jesus did not come to help out your life. Jesus came to take over your life. Get out of the way and let Him do what He came to do!

Get passionate about prayer! Learn to pray, dear sister. Prayer is simply speaking your heart to God. He cares about what you care about. For God, nothing is too big and nothing is too small. He told you in His Word to cast your cares upon Him because He cares for you (1 Peter 5:7). Be bold, be persistent, and be confident when you pray. James tells you that you do not have because you do not ask. You ask and don't receive because you ask with wrong motives. Make sure that what you are praying for lines up with what God's Word says. Pray His promises back to Him and claim them as your own. Have a specific place where you go to meet with God, to talk with Him and fellowship with Him. Pray, precious one, expecting answers. "*All* things you ask in prayer, believing, you *will* receive" (Matthew 21:22 NASB, emphasis added). God made you. God saved you. God raised you and seated you with Him in a heavenly place. He waits for you! He created you to have fellowship with you. Pray to Him. Talk to Him every day. He is all you need!

The hours you have invested in God's Word can never be taken from you. And because we have spent these hours together, none of us will ever be the same. We will no longer look at beauty the way we did in the past. We will never again make the mistake of thinking that beauty is skin-deep. We know now that true beauty, eternal beauty, comes from within.

I hate good-byes. I make relationships very deep, and I don't give them up easily. Even though we have not made this journey side by side, I have felt your joy, your sorrow, your pain, and your freedom as you were delivered from the bondage you have lived in for many years. I look forward to hearing from you when you visit Succeed and Lead's website and share with me the remarkable things God has done in you as you have journeyed with me. If you accepted Jesus Christ in this study, I would very much love to know about it! Anything that has been accomplished has been God's doing! We at Succeed and Lead want to get you connected to a body of believers so you can continue to grow and mature in Christ. If you and I do not have the opportunity to meet here, I will look forward to seeing you in heaven. I am very proud of you, sweet sister, but more importantly, God is proud of you!

Sometimes I say too much. There have been very few times when I have been at a loss for words. I talk for too long. I get too involved. I have so much I want to say to you before we part. There is so much I want you to know *right now!* But the Holy Spirit, my sweet teacher and Counselor, is reminding me that knowing Christ is a lifetime journey. No matter where you are in your journey, know this: strip off every sin, every weight, and run your race with endurance. Keep your eyes on Jesus, the author and finisher of your faith. I love you and look forward to hearing from you soon!

You are beautiful!

You are fearfully and wonderfully made!

You are fashioned!

You are designed to be like Him!

God has a beautiful plan for your life *if* you will do it His way!

Beautiful Memory Cards

Be Confident

Everything You Say

All Things Work

Unto Him Who Is Able

Trust in the Lord

I Urge You

For I Know

Uphold Me

Let Us Run the Race

Memory Cards

In the form of memory cards, I have included the nine foundational principles we have learned in the study. Cut them out and meditate on their messages. This will arm you and ready you for the fight that is ahead.

	T Trust in the Lord with all your heart and do not lean on your own understanding. In all your ways acknowledge Him and He will make your paths straight. Do not be wise in your own eyes. Fear the Lord and turn away from evil. —Proverbs 3:5–7 (NASB)
B Being confident of this, that He who began a good work in you will carry it on to completion until Jesus comes back. —Philippians 1:6 (NIV)	**I** I urge you, brothers and sisters, in view of God's mercy to offer your bodies as living sacrifices, holy and pleasing to God—this is your spiritual act of worship. Do not conform any longer to the pattern of this world, but be transformed by the renewing of your mind. Then you will be able to test and approve what God's will is—His good, pleasing and perfect will. —Romans 12:1–2 (NIV)

E	F
Everything you say must be good and helpful so that your words will be an encouragement to those who hear them. Do not use foul or abusive language. And do not bring sorrow to God's Holy Spirit by the way you live. Remember, He is the One who has identified you as His own, guaranteeing that you will be saved on the day of redemption. —Ephesians 4:29–32 (NLT)	"For I know the plans I have for you," declares the Lord, "plans to prosper you and not to harm you, plans to give you hope and a future. Then you will call upon Me and come and pray to Me, and I will listen to you. You will seek Me and find Me when you seek Me with all your heart." —Jeremiah 29:11–13 (NIV)
A	**U**
And we know that God causes all things to work together for the good of those who love God, to those who are called according to His purpose. —Romans 8:28 (NASB)	Uphold me with Your righteous right hand. I will not fear for You are with me. I will not anxiously look about, for You are my God. You will strengthen me. You will help me. —Isaiah 41:10 (NASB)
U	**L**
Unto Him who is able to do far more abundantly beyond all that we ask or think, according to the power that works within us, to Him be glory in the church and in Christ Jesus to all generations forever and ever. Amen. —Ephesians 3:20–21 (NASB)	Let us strip off every weight that slows us down, especially the sin that so easily hinders our progress. Let us run with endurance the race that God has set before us. We do this by keeping our eyes on Jesus, on Whom our faith depends from start to finish. —Hebrews 12:1–2 (NLT)

The BEAUTIFUL Club

Beautiful was a manual originally written for teens and tweens. As God brought to my mind Christian sisters whom I love and respect for their walk with the Lord, I asked those sisters to read through the study to give me godly counsel about its content. They all shared one central thought about the study: this study is for every Christian who desires to have a strong foundation on which to build her life. This being said, one vision that God has given me is to have BEAUTIFUL clubs in every community all around the country.

Each club would have a mature, seasoned mentor who would lead her group in the interactive study. I shared my vision in the "About the Study" section, but I will repeat it here. I am asking God to raise up an army of young women who will love God with all their heart, mind, soul, and strength; women who will arm themselves with the sword of the Spirit and the shield of faith; women who will march with me into the Enemy's camp and take back what he has stolen; women who will be pure because God is pure; women who will stand for truth because God is truth. I am asking God for warriors—mighty warriors who will join with me to change the direction of this next generation. Evil is becoming more evil. Christianity is under attack like never before. Satan uses isolation to devour and destroy.

Young women need a banner beneath which to march. They need to know that they are loved unconditionally. They need to be with other young women who have a heart for God. They need to know that they are not alone, that we are in this fight together. All of us need accountability if we are to succeed in our walk with Christ. I cherish your prayers, sweet sisters. Pray with me that God will raise up these mentors and leaders to help build this army of women who will change the world.

Ideas for Hosting a Beautiful Club

1. Meet regularly at the same time and location. Attendees will be able to invite their friends if they know when the club meets. The consistency will help you be able to plan for the time together. This type of stability is often a missing piece in the lives of the girls you will be reaching.

2. Enlist the prayer warriors around you to pray for God's presence and against Satan's influence. Petition God to prepare their hearts for the truth they will hear. Ask the Holy Spirit to speak through you with power and authority.

3. Make sure you have positive contemporary Christian music playing as the girls arrive. Music with a strong, positive message will set the atmosphere and prepare each attendee's heart to receive God's Word. You can visit our website at www.succeedandlead.org to find artists and songs that are appropriate for the meeting.

4. Have a prayer box available, into which attendees can, after writing down specific problems and challenges they may be facing, place their petitions. Explain to them that they do not have to put their name on the prayer request if they do not want to. God knows all and sees all. As we voice each need to God, He meets each need personally and individually. We may be in a crowd of hundreds, but we live in the presence of One.

5. Choose two or three young women you have observed who know how to love people and who know how to have an intimate relationship with Christ. Have them at the meeting to watch for those girls who may feel intimidated or fearful about being in a room with new people. It is important that every girl feel loved and accepted. This will disarm Satan and allow the Holy Spirit to have free rein to move and work.

6. Be mindful to start on time and end on time. Everyone has made an effort to fit this study into their busy schedule. Close when you said you would. Always start with prayer and end with prayer. Go over the assignment to be completed by the next meeting time.

The Succeed and Lead Organization

Building Generations of Sincere Faith

Mission: To become an example of Christ by handling accurately the Word of Truth and to build generations of sincere faith by holding that example and guarding the treasure that has been entrusted to us.

Succeed: Set the standard. Be the example.

"Be diligent to present yourself approved to God as a workman who does not need to be ashamed, handling accurately the Word of Truth" (2 Timothy 2:15 NASB).

Lead: Retain the standard. Hold the example.

"Retain the standard of sound words which you have heard from me, in the faith and love which are in Christ Jesus. Guard through the Holy Spirit who dwells in us the treasure which has been entrusted to you" (2 Timothy 1:13–14 NASB).

Please visit us at www.succeedandlead.org.

About the Author

Sheila Hoffman was born in Memphis, Tennessee, to a mother who was told she would never have children. Surprise! We serve a God of surprises and second chances. After a mere nineteen months of hearing that pronouncement, Sheila's mother was given a bouncing baby girl. The Murphree house would be changed forever. Their life would never be the same. The father was excited because God had answered the second half of a prayer he had prayed many years before as he lay dying on a battlefield in Korea. The promise he whispered was, "God, if You will let me live, get me back home, and give me a family, then I will live for You and teach my family how to live for You as long as I have breath." Sheila's dad kept that promise to God and introduced her at the age of ten to the One who took her sin and canceled her debt. Jesus paid a debt He did not owe because Sheila owed a debt she could not pay.

Jesus not only touched Sheila that night but also changed her forever. He put a new song in her heart, a hymn of praise to her God. She began singing and serving in her local church. She attended Union University in Jackson, Tennessee, where she studied music. She would travel every weekend with a revival team to sing and to minister God's Word.

After two years, God called her back home to Memphis, where she studied and received a nursing degree from Baptist School of Nursing. It was there she met her husband, Steve. They were married in 1977. God blessed them with their first baby girl in 1979—and then their second, and then their third, and finally their fourth bouncing bundle of joy. It was in this world of zits and makeup, boys and raging hormones, that Sheila would learn that God is bigger than any problem, any challenge, and any circumstance. *He is enough!*

Sheila now resides in Birmingham, Alabama, with her husband, Steve. They are active members of Gardendale First Baptist Church. She is the proud grandmother (Mimi) of three boys and—yep, you guessed it—six little women. The drama and emotion continues, and so does Sheila's love for and complete dependence on God's Word. One of her greatest joys is watching her faith, which she passed on to her daughters, being passed onto the next generation. It is from this experience that God has birthed the ministry Succeed and Lead: Building Generations of Sincere Faith. Sheila writes and teaches to people of every generation, young and old. She realizes that no matter where you are in life, you must succeed in your journey to become like Christ if you are going to lead others.

Prayer

_____

_____

_____

_____

_____

_____

_____

_____

_____

_____

_____

_____

_____

_____

_____

_____

_____

Petition

Praise

_____

_____

_____

_____

_____

_____

_____

_____

_____

_____

_____

_____

_____

_____

_____

_____

_____

_____

_____

Printed in the United States
By Bookmasters